MW01244126

THE
HAPPY JOURNAL

Make Your Happiness

Penny Press Publishing Co.

DEDICATED

To your happiness

Preface

About 10 years ago I was introduced to the idea of the law of attraction; a concept born out of the newly developed law of quantum physics. There are hundreds of books on the subject you can read if you are not familiar with the term. However, a very basic explanation of this law is that 'thoughts become things'. What this means is, whatever you think about is what you create in your life. One of the keys to success, with using the law of attraction, is to focus on positive thoughts, and thoughts that feel good, in order to receive more good things into your life.

When I came across the law of attraction, I was looking to attract things into my life that would make me feel happy – like lots of money – but according to the law of attraction, I had to feel happy first to get the things I wanted. *What?* I thought, *I have to feel good to get the things I want, so I can feel good? If I could feel good anyway, then I would not want the things that would make me feel happy.* This was very confusing and almost seemed farcical. I wanted certain things because I was miserably unhappy and just wanted to be happy. I knew there was this whole "happiness comes from the inside" thing, but what does that even mean? I already liked myself as a person; I just didn't like being poor and miserable. I wanted to 'attract' things to make me feel good.

I became sucked into a Law of Attraction vortex: obsessively visualizing what I wanted, creating vision boards, while watching every thought I had because 'thoughts become things', and I didn't want more miserable things in my life.

Ten years went by and I was still not where I had been 'thinking' myself into being. I was still unhappy.

Since then, I have evolved into a better place. I would not want to be the same person I was 10 years ago. I have grown and even fulfilled my lifelong dream of becoming a fiction author. Yes, I have finally done it! However, even though I had fulfilled a lifelong dream I was still not happy, and that realization was the final straw. I had achieved my dream job and I was still unhappy. I was devastated, confused, and very angry.

Thankfully, I was also persistent and one day I decided the only way I could really be happy would be to embrace everything, within my control, that could make me happy. I decided to sit down and make a list of 10 things that made my heart smile. I came up with writing, home decorating, chocolate, my family, movies, learning, music, inspiring words and creating ideas, and then the list flowed over with even more items. I decided I was going to participate – be PROACTIVE – in doing these things every day. So I looked at the list of topics and added all the different things I could do.

What I found was that life would, kind of, get in the

way of actually doing what I loved. Weirdly, despite this, I found myself feeling happy anyway. I realized all I had to do every morning was look at this long list of things I love, and I would start the day feeling good. Each morning I would wake up excited to look at my list, which by now had turned into a journal. It was then, for the first time ever, it happened – I was happy. A feeling of contentment swept through me and I had a smile in my heart.

Now, here's the thing, I am a single mom of two daughters. I don't have time to sit around and be Gandhi. I know there are a lot of gurus out there who have been fortunate enough to acquire financial freedom early in their lives. They may have had a spouse to take care of things, while they made their way in the world, or maybe they didn't have a spouse or kids at all, but they go about telling you how you can do it! Indeed, you can, but it can be far more challenging when you have filled your life with numerous other obligations that make it difficult to find the time AND energy to establish your financial freedom.

There was nobody there to take care of things for me. It was all up to me, a single mom working late nights, and early mornings, only to find I still wasn't happy. It all seemed like work, work, work…and it was making me miserable. I just had a feeling it did not need to take all this work, there had to be a 'smarter – not harder' approach I could follow. That was when I discovered all I had to do was make a list and look at it, at least once a day, to FINALLY be able to create the happiness I was looking for. Well, Hallelujah!

There are many of us who have overwhelmingly busy and demanding lives, and it may feel as if you don't have time to do this journal thing. I'm here to tell you that you do. Even if you just make a list of at least 10 things at the beginning of your journal and take 10 seconds each morning to look at this happy list, it can make a huge difference. That difference will accelerate you towards finding some happy feelings.

There is something about creating something with your hands that feeds your heart. You need to make time, like I have, to sit down each morning, or evening, and look at your HAPPY JOURNAL. The biggest reason you NEED to create your happiness is because it affects everyone around you. I knew I owed it to my daughters, family, friends, and the person in the grocery line, to be happy. It was my responsibility to create my happiness proactively, so I could be the best me for everyone I met. My happiness is not just about me – it's about everyone.

~~~

THE HAPPY JOURNAL

THE HAPPY JOURNAL

HOW TO USE THE HAPPY JOURNAL

STEP 1:
On the first couple of pages of your journal, make a list of everything you can think of that makes you feel happy. Get started and remember you can always add more items to the list later. This list will get you started thinking of all the different things you can put in your happy journal!

STEP 2:
Start creating your happy! This journal is already filled with quotes about happiness, ideas to get you thinking, and blank pages so you can add any, and all, things that make you feel happy – see HAPPY JOURNAL IDEAS on the next page for suggestions. (*Note: Some pens can bleed through the pages so be sure to test them first.*)

STEP 3:
Once you have completed your happy journal keep it somewhere accessible, like your nightstand, and flip through it every morning and/or night. This is the key to being proactive in creating a happy lifestyle!

~ ~ ~

THE HAPPY JOURNAL

HAPPY JOURNAL IDEAS:

- Write down your favorite memories, quotes, affirmations, poems, etc. Try using different colored pens. *(Note: Some pens can bleed through the pages so be sure to test them first.)*
- Add photos to your journal. These can be photos of loved ones or pictures you find online of art you like, your favorite quotes and other images. Get them printed onto photo paper at your local photo shop, and then stick them into the book.
- Cut out words of wisdom from your favorite books.
- Cut out pictures from your favorite magazines.
- Add drawings or create drawings/doodles yourself.
- Get various scrapbooking stickers and/or cut-outs to add to the pages.
- Pick a page and stick in everything that is in your favorite color.
- Add items that spark great memories; ticket stubs from movies, concerts, or sporting events.
- Stick in fun things like candy wrappers, CD/DVD covers, food/beverage labels, travel flyers, etc.
- Have fun and add pictures (or whatever) of things you dream of being, doing, or having: a nice car, fancy house, big trip, or being a rock star. The idea of having something can

sometimes be more fun than actually having it – so put it in the journal! However, keep in mind this is not about 'things', but rather being proactive in creating happy feelings through them as visuals.

Follow us on Pinterest for more creative ideas on what to include. We have created various boards we update daily, which are designed especially to be used with THE HAPPY JOURNAL!

www.Pinterest.com/PennyPressBooks

However, remember these are only ideas about what to include. You do not have to spend money, or a lot of time, to get great results from your own Happy Journal. My first journal only had words cut out from different books and things I wrote in black pen. It was not at all fancy, or pretty, but it still transformed my life. This is your journal…you must always do what is right for you!

~ ~ ~

THE HAPPY JOURNAL

THE HAPPY JOURNAL

HOLD ME EVERY DAY.
-The Happy Journal

THE
HAPPY JOURNAL

Make Your Happiness

Penny Press Publishing Co.

THE HAPPY JOURNAL

MY HAPPY LIST

List anything, and everything, you can think of that creates a positive feeling; from a cup of great coffee to being a rock star. It doesn't matter how little or big these things are, if they put a smile on your face and zing in your heart when you think about them, then write them down! Start with AT LEAST 10 items — you can always add more later.

1.

2.

3.

4.

5.

6.

7.

8.

9.

10.

11.

12.

13.

14.

15.

16.

17.

18.

19.

20.

21.

22.

23.

24.

25.

Now get creating! ...

THE HAPPY JOURNAL

Don't be afraid to give yourself
everything you ever wanted in life.

I dream of having…

THE HAPPY JOURNAL

THE HAPPY JOURNAL

It's not about the happy endings, it's about the story.

Happiness is…

~ ~ ~

THE HAPPY JOURNAL

THE HAPPY JOURNAL

Love is the master key that opens
the gates of happiness.

My loves…

THE HAPPY JOURNAL

THE HAPPY JOURNAL

The greatest happiness
is family happiness.

Family...

THE HAPPY JOURNAL

THE HAPPY JOURNAL

Happiness is an inside job.

What I love most about me…

THE HAPPY JOURNAL

You can't buy happiness. But you can buy donuts. And that's kind of the same thing.

Things that make me smile…

THE HAPPY JOURNAL

THE HAPPY JOURNAL

It's not selfish to love yourself, take care of yourself, and to CREATE your happiness. It's necessary.

Things I love to do...

~ ~ ~

THE HAPPY JOURNAL

Happiness is the secret to all beauty.

What makes me beautiful…

THE HAPPY JOURNAL

Be happy for this moment.
This moment in your life.

My most precious moment…

THE HAPPY JOURNAL

Happiness is a conscious choice,
not an automatic response.

I choose to be happy by…

THE HAPPY JOURNAL

Happiness is when you feel good about yourself without feeling the need for anyone else's approval.

I feel good when…

THE HAPPY JOURNAL

Smile and the world smiles with you.

My heart smiles when…

THE HAPPY JOURNAL

Happiness is a way of travel,
not a destination.

My inspirations…

THE HAPPY JOURNAL

THE HAPPY JOURNAL

You don't need a reason for doing everything in your life. Do it because you want to. Because it's fun. Because it makes you feel happy.

Things I want to do…

THE HAPPY JOURNAL

To be happy learn from those
who are happy.

Those who I learn from…

THE HAPPY JOURNAL

THE HAPPY JOURNAL

Be thankful, whatever the situation you are in. Because happiness will never come to those who fail to appreciate.

I am so grateful for…

THE HAPPY JOURNAL

THE HAPPY JOURNAL

Wake up each morning with a great
desire to live joyfully.

Things that bring me joy...

THE HAPPY JOURNAL

THE HAPPY JOURNAL

Happiness is not something you get in life.
Happiness is something that you bring to life.

How I bring happiness…

THE HAPPY JOURNAL

THE HAPPY JOURNAL

The happiness of your life depends on
the quality of your thoughts.

My positive thoughts…

THE HAPPY JOURNAL

THE HAPPY JOURNAL

Action may not bring happiness, but there is no happiness without action.

My happy action plan...

THE HAPPY JOURNAL

THE HAPPY JOURNAL

Happiness is always knocking on your door, you just gotta let it in.

How to open my happy door...

THE HAPPY JOURNAL

The happiest people don't have the best of everything, they just make the best of everything.

The best things in my life…

THE HAPPY JOURNAL

Always find a reason to smile.

Things that make me smile…

THE HAPPY JOURNAL

THE HAPPY JOURNAL

FINAL THOUGHTS....

LIVE SIMPLY

DREAM BIG

BE GRATEFUL

GIVE LOVE

LAUGH LOTS

INSPIRE

BE INSPIRED

CREATE YOUR JOY

AND BE HAPPY!

THE HAPPY JOURNAL

ABOUT THE AUTHOR

Heidi A. Thatcher is the creator of *The Happy Journal* and *A Penny for Your Thoughts* gift book series. She is a public speaker, an author of numerous psychological fiction books, and has a passion for promoting the power of positive thinking!

THE HAPPY JOURNAL

.

Be sure to visit **www.PennyPressBOOKS.com**
For all published and coming soon books.

Check out our *A Penny for Your Thoughts* gift books!

A Penny for Your Thoughts: ON MARRIAGE

A Penny for Your Thoughts: ON PARENTHOOD

A Penny for Your Thoughts: ON GRADUATIION

A Penny for Your Thoughts: ON RETIREMENT

A Penny for Your Thoughts: ON BIRTHDAYS

A Penny for Your Thoughts: ON HEALING

A Penny for Your Thoughts: ON THE HOLIDAYS

A Penny for Your Thoughts: ON A NEW HOME

A Penny for Your Thoughts: ON THE ARMED FORCES

A Penny for Your Thoughts gift books are comprised of a selection of both famous, and not-so-famous, quotes and sayings. What makes these books special, however, are the blank pages waiting to be filled in by family and friends. It's an end-table book and keepsake that can be enjoyed over and over again.

THE HAPPY JOURNAL

Made in the USA
Middletown, DE
25 April 2023

29220149R00073